HEAL YOUR
Mind,
CHANGE YOUR
Life

FROM INTERNAL CONFLICT
TO LIVING A PURPOSEFUL LIFE

Dina M. Celestin

WESTBOW
PRESS®
A DIVISION OF THOMAS NELSON
& ZONDERVAN

WestBow Press books may be ordered through
booksellers or by contacting:

WestBow Press
A Division of Thomas Nelson & Zondervan
1663 Liberty Drive
Bloomington, IN 47403
www.westbowpress.com
844-714-3454

Scripture taken from the New King James Version® Copyright ©
1982 by Thomas Nelson. Used by permission. All rights reserved.

ISBN: 978-1-6642-4870-0 (sc)
ISBN: 978-1-6642-4869-4 (e)

Library of Congress Control Number: 2021922198

Print information available on the last page.

WestBow Press rev. date: 11/24/2021

ACKNOWLEDGMENTS

I first want to acknowledge my heavenly Father for blessing me with my different talents/gifts, the main one being creativity. I am eternally grateful for such a magical gift, and my life's goal is to represent my Creator in the best light possible.

I must acknowledge my loving husband, Marc Celestin Jr., who has played such a huge role in my journey toward healing. Thank you for loving me as I work through my traumas, and for never being judgmental.

To my loves, Jazmine Joy Celestin and Marcus Iman Celestin, you are the reasons why I work so hard. My goal is to leave a positive legacy behind that the both of you can reap the benefits of long after I'm gone. I pray that you'll always remember that your mommy loves you more than life itself.

I must honor the memory of my friend Pastor Anderson St. Louis, who made it his life's mission to encourage, motivate, and spread joy to those around him, regardless of what life threw at him. I'm grateful for our conversations and the encouragement he always gave me to step out on faith and do what the Lord puts on my heart to do. Rest in paradise, Andy! Until we meet again.

To my parents Pierre & Raymonde Theodore, thank you for giving me everything you could. I appreciate the gift of your love, and I will never take that for granted.

Many blessings,
Dina M. Celestin

CONTENTS

INTRODUCTION

The process of writing this book has been a labor of love that spans over five years in the making. It was birthed from my own personal journey toward living the purposeful life I now know I was created to live. The details outlined in this book have helped me face the internal conflict that kept me from living out my purpose. By using the declarations, prayers, words of affirmation, and so forth that I've now written inside this book, I was able to release my past hurt while figuring out how to manage my emotions. The words written have been very therapeutic and served as the bridge to help me embrace the life that awaited me beyond all the hurt and pain I harbored inside for years.

I decided that I no longer wanted to view life through the lens of the hurt and pain I once had. Those feelings kept me in a negative mindset for over a decade, and I knew it was time for a change. I held on to negativity for as long as I could remember until the day I decided to let go. One by one, I started thinking of the origin of every one of my negative thoughts. By pinpointing where each came from, I was able to face them, and eventually I started writing down those thoughts, along with daily steps to take to help me start letting them go. In this book are the steps that

I believe were divinely revealed to me to help me in my journey toward healing my heart and relieving my mind. Applying these techniques has helped me tremendously on my journey to a more enjoyable life.

My prayer is that this book would serve as a guide to help you through the process of healing by providing techniques to aid in releasing the different concepts and crippling mindsets that no longer serve you. These techniques will serve as tools to help you clear through the clutter to start living a purposeful and enjoyable life. We have all dealt with hurt and pain of some sort, but not all of us take the necessary steps to properly heal. So this book is here to help you start the healing process.

This book will help you start taking proactive steps to release the things from your past that hinder you from moving forward. But first, you must ask yourself if you're truly ready to start the healing process, as it requires you to dig deep. It would be wise for you to search your heart before you decide to start this winding road toward wholeness.

"Heal Your Mind, Change Your Life" can be read on your own, but in my humble opinion, it would be more beneficial to you if read in a small group setting. I pray that you will read and apply the words in this book to your life. By doing so, I believe your life will never be the same.

You may not have been responsible for your trauma, but you are fully responsible for your healing. So, let's start the journey toward your healing together!

1

YOU ARE ENOUGH

I praise you, for I am fearfully and
wonderfully made. Wonderful are your
works; my soul knows it very well.

—Psalm 139:14 (ESV)

I HAVE ALWAYS had a deep longing to feel loved and
accepted and to gain a sense of belonging. I'm sure many of
you can relate. We as human beings crave deep, meaningful
connections with others, and that's a normal human desire
to have. What isn't normal is the feeling that you have to
alter who you are at your core and compromise your values
in order to maintain those connections. You shouldn't have
to change your responses on certain topics or even change
the way you speak to fit in anywhere, and if you do, it's time
to evaluate the way you view yourself. Forming meaningful
relationships isn't always easy, but you shouldn't feel the need
to become a different person in order to maintain them.

The day you take the time to get to know yourself and
what sets you apart from everyone else, you'll realize that

you are enough. Those who truly love you will accept you, flaws and all, so there's no need to wear a mask. Whether you realize it or not, we've all worn a mask at some point of in our lives. But the day you choose to unmask yourself, you'll experience an unexplainable freedom that can never be stripped away from you. Only then will you realize that you have everything you need to succeed dwelling on the inside of you.

You have been created by the Most High with a specific purpose, and it's up to you to discover what that is. Once you discover who you are and why, you're obligated to fulfill those things that only you can. Everything from your past will serve as a guide to aid in fulfilling your purpose. You don't have to walk with your head hung down—wear your scares proudly and share your story. Because that is what sets you apart from everyone else. Know that as you share your story, others will find healing. Every tough situation and every painful place was all in preparation to help you pull others out of the struggles you've previously overcome.

Because of your background and the hurdles you've had to leap over, there's a group of people in the world whom only you can reach. As you begin to walk in your purpose and share your truth, your voice will resonate with those from similar backgrounds to yours, and it'll be up to you to lead the way to the path of healing. Just remember that your tribe is waiting on you to realize that you are enough to handle the task that lies ahead.

Grab hold of your new identity by choosing to forget what others have said about you or what you have said to yourself. Make the choice to stop self-sabotaging, and show yourself more grace and kindness. You are a rare jewel perfectly created to reflect the goodness of your Creator. You are truly one of a kind, and there will never be another you like you on the face of this earth. Let that sink in. The Creator thought you were so important that He took the time to perfect the person you are. With your flaws and all, you are loved. You are radiant, so don't be afraid to share who you really are with the world around you.

NOTES

YOU ARE ENOUGH:
A BOLD DECLARATION

I declare that I am enough.

With my flaws and all, I am enough.

I'm not yet who I want to be, but I am enough.

I have everything I need to fulfill my purpose; yes, I am enough.

I have the wisdom of God, so yes, I am enough.

There's nothing I can't do; I am enough.

I may have failed in the past, but I am enough.

I will keep pushing through because I know that I am enough.

Today I boldly stand in my truth, and I dare to believe that I am enough.

Amen.

CONTINUING YOUR JOURNEY TOWARD KNOWING THAT YOU ARE ENOUGH

Love Letter

Write a love letter to yourself. In this letter, highlight the different things you love about yourself. Write out what you think would be missing in this world if you weren't in it. Write down at least three kind words you can say about yourself when your insecurities start to creep in.

Daily Declaration

I am beautiful. (I am handsome—for male readers.)

I am kind.

I am intelligent.

I am loved.

I am a child of God.

So I will not fail.

Thought-Provoking Questions

1. What sets you apart from others?

_____

_____

_____

_____

2. What is your life's purpose? How will you go about achieving it?

_____

_____

_____

_____

Congratulations!

You have taken the 1st step towards changing
your life!
Keep going!
A life worth living awaits you ahead.

Love,
Dina M. Celestin

2

THE POWER OF FORGIVENESS

And when you stand praying, if
you hold anything against anyone,
forgive them, so that your Father in
heaven may forgive you your sins.

—Mark 11:25 (NIV)

THE ABILITY TO forgive has the power to transform your life in an overwhelmingly positive way. Forgiveness will help free you of the burden of carrying around hurt, pain, anger, and anything else that weighs you down. It will allow you to gain the freedom to live out your God-given purpose.

Although forgiveness is essential to restoring peace of mind, it's not always easy. When a loved one or someone you trusted betrays you, it cuts deep. But I've found it especially difficult to forgive myself for self-afflicted pain caused by the way I allowed people to treat me in the past. How many of you can relate? Forgiving yourself is a tough space to be in because you spend every waking moment with the "I should have known better" phrase lingering in your mind. Personally, that's one of the toughest hurtles I've had to overcome. But when I learned to extend some grace and kindness to myself, I not only forgave myself for past mistakes and failures, but I gained the ability to forgive others.

For a long time, I would brush off the feelings I had that were rooted in unforgiveness, but at the end of the day, the feelings still haunted me. Oxforddictionaries.com defines the verb *forgive* as the ability "to stop feeling angry or resentful toward (someone) for an offence, flaw or mistake." So, the key component to true forgiveness is to *stop feeling* the same way you once felt about some of life's inevitable misfortunes. Once you can take a step back and look at the big picture, you'll see the different ways that unforgiveness has negatively affected your life. The thought alone should serve as a stepping-stone toward the choice to start forgiving.

It's been often said that forgiveness has more to do with your personal healing and peace of mind than it has to do with another person. I'll go a step further and say that the ability to forgive is directly linked to your ability to achieve your life's purpose. Forgiveness is a powerful tool, and with it you have the power to transcend over everything and everyone that has previously kept you bound.

You must make a conscious decision to let go of the cancerous feeling of unforgiveness and create new daily habits that remind you of your new decision. The decision to forgive is a path that should be walked daily, and each time a thought tries to challenge your decision, train yourself to think of the many times you have been in need of a little forgiveness. If you're real with yourself, that will help humble you enough to give what you have often needed: a little forgiveness.

NOTES

FORGIVE AND RELEASE EXERCISE

Keep in mind you can't give what you don't have. If you haven't given yourself the gift of forgiveness, you won't have anything to pull from to extend that gift to anyone else. So, start this exercise by forgiving yourself; then you can move forward and use this tool to forgive others.

Repeat the following steps as many times as needed to rid your heart of every person you need to forgive. Fill in the first blank with the name of the person who has hurt you and fill in the second blank with everything associated with the hurt. You can also write these down if you don't want to say them aloud.

1. Sit with your eyes closed and your heart opened.

2. Think back to the person/situation you've been hurt by.

3. Allow yourself to go back to that place of hurt and pain.

4. Allow your mind to remember all the details of the situation.

5. Allow yourself to *feel* that pain again.

Right where you have been hurt, you will experience your greatest victory.

6. Take a deep breath. Breathe in all the strength you can muster up, and when you're ready, say aloud, "I choose to forgive _____ for _____.

7. Then breathe some more, pushing out all the hurt, pain, and negative energy that have been preventing you from moving forward.

Congratulations! By doing this you have just taken back your power!

These steps can be done as often as needed to cleanse yourself of all the negative energy surrounding unforgiveness.

CONTINUING YOUR JOURNEY OF FORGIVENESS

Morning Prayer

God, I thank You for allowing me to get to this place of self-awareness. I ask that You please reveal to me the emotional wounds that cause me to isolate myself from others. I'm asking You to please do a deep work in me so I can experience the healing I so desperately need. Please allow me to see the origin of my pain and give me the necessary strength to continually forgive and release the source of that pain. I no longer want to be weighed down by the burden of unforgiveness.

Thought-Provoking Questions

1. How did God show up in your journey toward forgiveness today?

   _____

   _____

   _____

   _____

2. How did you recognize it was Him?

   _____

   _____

   _____

   _____

DAILY REMINDER

People react differently to things that are out of their control. So just remember, most of the time what they're saying or doing is not personal. A lot of times you are not the real target; you just happen to be there at that moment. Protect yourself and move away from the situation, but don't internalize or dwell on their words. Always choose to forgive.

Thought-Provoking Questions

1. Have you ever lashed out at someone out of frustration?

_____

_____

_____

_____

2. Be honest. Was your issue really with that person?

_____

_____

_____

_____

DAILY ENCOURAGEMENT

You may not have thought of it, but some people go through life with the weight of what others have said about them on their shoulders. They go through their daily routines, but each time they hear something that sounds like what's already going on in their heads, it triggers them and causes them to lash out. Today I encourage you to give them a pass. Not a pass to mistreat and abuse you but a pass of nonjudgment. We're all struggling with something, so instead of passing judgment, try approaching people you meet with compassion.

Thought-Provoking Questions

1. What have you learned about forgiveness?

    _____

    _____

    _____

    _____

2. How will you apply what you've learned to your daily life?

    _____

    _____

    _____

    _____

Congratulations!

You have taken the 2nd step towards changing
your life!
You can & you will!
Your life can be much more enjoyable if you keep
going.

Love,
Dina M. Celestin

3

LETTING DOWN YOUR GUARD

I can do all things through Christ
who gives me strength.

—Philippians 4:13 (NIV)

LETTING DOWN YOUR guard can be a challenge, and keeping your guard up can be a challenge, so make your choice. We all have different defense mechanisms to prevent ourselves from getting hurt, and keeping our guard up is just one of them. But the problem with that is it also prevents you from forming deep and meaningful relationships, which are important for an overall more enjoyable life.

Honestly, choosing to consistently let my guard down has been one of the most difficult things for me to practice on my life's journey. After years of hurt and disappointment, it became difficult to trust because I feared getting hurt yet again. It can be challenging, but by letting down your guard, setting boundaries, and slowly allowing yourself to trust again, you are opening yourself up to receive true joy. Through my personal experiences, I've learned that letting your guard down allows you the opportunity to form better relationships. It also helps you to be more loving and empathetic to those around you.

Letting your guard down and trusting again has the power to change your life. You may not have been solely responsible for the hurt, but you are solely responsible to seek out your healing. Think of all the deep and meaningful relationships that await you. It all starts by first making room for them. I encourage you to open up and welcome healing and wholeness into your heart.

NOTES

A PRAYER TO HELP WITH LETTING DOWN YOUR GUARD

Heavenly Father, please help me learn how to let my guard down. I am ready to start letting others in, and I realize that this can't be done while my guard is still up. Please help me tear down the walls that I've built and help me replace them with boundaries instead. I believe that all things work together for my good, and I choose to trust that my heart is in the right hands—Yours. I refuse to believe that You will allow my heart to get into the wrong hands.

In Jesus's name I pray. Amen.

CONTINUING YOUR JOURNEY OF LETTING DOWN YOUR GUARD

Daily Declaration

Today I will allow myself to view things through the lens of positivity.

I choose to welcome new people, new experiences, and new adventures into my life.

I will not project my own fears and insecurities onto others.

Everyone is not out to destroy me.

There is plenty of good in the world.

So today I make room to receive all the good I have coming my way.

Thought-Provoking Questions

1a. Have you been able to let your guard down today?

_____

_____

1b. If so, how did you feel afterward?

_____

_____

1c. If not, what do you feel is holding you back from doing so?

_____

_____

Congratulations!

You have taken the 3rd step towards changing
your life!
You got this!
You've come too far to give up now.

Love,
Dina M. Celestin

4

HOW TO TRUST AGAIN

Trust in the Lord forever, for the
Lord God is an everlasting rock.

—Isaiah 26:4 (ESV)

I CHOOSE TO believe that we are all born with an innate ability to trust. As children, we naturally develop the ability to trust through our relationships with our parents. We count on them for everything, and we *trust* that they will always be there for us. No one had to teach you that; you formed your own conclusions based on the time spent together. The amount of time spent with your parents helped you determine the level of trust you have for them. During the time spent together, you're able to conclude that they will always be there to love, protect, and provide for you.

But what happens when that trust has been stripped away from you? What happens when you didn't get the opportunity to develop an ability to trust? It becomes nearly impossible to navigate through life being able to fully trust others when this ability is somehow underdeveloped. It's even more difficult when the ability to trust has somehow been destroyed; it affects the way you trust people in every relationship you encounter, whether it be cordial or romantic.

There are a lot of misconceptions about trust, but one that cannot be denied is that trust is not given; it is earned. The ability to trust can only be gained through spending quality time with the one whose trust you'd like to gain. Through quality time, you will feel their spirit, and they will feel yours, and if you're supposed to be in each other's life, you'll feel that undeniable connection that will give you the ability to trust them. This is true of any relationship, whether it's a friendship, a marriage, or any other relationship in between. No trustworthy relationship can be established without spending quality one-on-one time and having open and honest conversations with each other. This needs to be a time where you're able to let your guard down and be your authentic self. During this time, you'll be able to see if the person you're trying to connect with can love and appreciate you with no filters.

NOTES

TRUST EXERCISE

1. Sit down and close your eyes.

2. Think back to the last time in your life when you were able to fully trust someone.

3. Once you have that image in your mind, take a deep breath and allow yourself to feel like you did during that time.

4. Once you're comfortable enough, say aloud, "Today I choose to trust again"—take in a deep breath, get a clear image in your mind of how you feel around a person when you trust them, and then exhale your feelings of doubt—"the same way I did when _____."

Hold on to the image of the last time you truly trusted someone, and let that be your guide to recognize what trust looks and feels like. Repeat as many times as you need to in order to get your image of trust in your mind.

CONTINUING YOUR JOURNEY TO TRUST AGAIN

Daily Declaration of Trust

Today I choose to trust the path that has been set before me.

I choose to look on the bright side of life and turn my back on all darkness.

I choose to let my light shine brighter than it has ever shone before.

I choose to believe that others have my best interest at heart unless proven otherwise.

I choose to trust as if I've never been hurt before.

I trust that everyone who enters my life enters on purpose for a purpose.

I trust that God will reveal to me those who have entered my life with the wrong intentions.

Thought-Provoking Questions

1. Why do you find it so difficult to trust? (Be as in-depth as possible.)

   _____

   _____

   _____

   _____

2a. Do you trust that God has your best interest at heart?

_____

_____

_____

_____

2b. If you find it difficult to trust, what do you feel is holding you back from doing so?

_____

_____

_____

_____

Congratulations!

You have taken the 4th step towards changing
your life!
You're almost there!
You've come a long way, celebrate your progress.

Love,
Dina M. Celestin

5

LIVING FEARLESSLY

For God has not given us a spirit
of fear, but of power and of
love and of a sound mind.

—2 Timothy 1:7 (NKJV)

HAVE YOU GIVEN yourself the freedom to live fearlessly? What you think of yourself truly matters because it'll help determine how you move through life. Fear can be crippling if you let it be, and it's the main thing that has the power to keep you from reaching your God-given destiny.

Fear tells you that you can't do it, you won't make it, or you don't have enough to achieve that thing you've been thinking of doing. Fear has the power to keep you stuck in a place you hate just because you're too afraid of the unknown. So, I invite you to take back the power you've once given over to fear.

If you take a step back and look at the bigger picture, you'll realize that through the steps that you've already done in this book, you have gained the necessary skills to now walk fearlessly toward the life you want for yourself. You have learned that you are enough, so you now know that you have everything you need to succeed right inside you. You have learned the importance of forgiveness and have gained some tools to help you on your daily journey toward forgiveness. You have also learned how to effectively let your guard down and set up boundaries that help you stay emotionally safe instead. You have learned how to start trusting again by spending quality time with those who are worthy of your time. So, you have unconsciously been working to reach this point where you can now live fearlessly.

Much like everything else we've discussed in this book, living fearlessly is a choice. You may not choose your fears, but you choose whether you let them control you. See, you could absolutely hate where you are in life and still choose to stay there, simply because of fear and the hold it has on your mind. Fear says, "Stay here. I know it's not where you want to be, but at least it's safe." In the meantime, you're safe, but you're unhappy; you're safe, but you're unfulfilled; you're safe, but you're not challenging yourself to become a better version of you. But the day you decide to step out in faith, fear has no choice but to move aside and let you through. You may still hear its whispers, but as you keep on walking, the voice of fear will decrease over time.

The secret to overcoming fear each time is to consistently seek to overcome the very things that make you fearful. Those fears try to prevent you from going after your dreams, but if you keep on going, you'll one day look back at your life and realize that you're living the fearless life you've always imagined living. God will never lead you astray; He will be there to guide you every step of the way through your life's journey, if you let Him.

NOTES

A BOLD DECLARATION
A COMPILATION OF 2 TIMOTHY
1:7 AND 1 PETER 5:7

Today I claim the mind of Christ as my own.

Today I am reminded that God did not give me a spirit of fear.

Today I declare that God gave me power, love, and a sound mind.

Today I choose to believe that God is on my side, so I will not fail.

Today I choose to walk in the strength of the Lord and cast all my fears on
Him and Him alone.

Amen.

CONTINUING YOUR JOURNEY TO LIVING FEARLESSLY

Daily Reminder

There's never been a problem that doesn't have a solution. There's never been a fear that can't be conquered, and there's never been a barrier that can't be moved. It only takes a little hard work, determination, and the willingness to never give up, even when it might get difficult.

Exercise

1. Take out a piece of paper and a pen.

2. Write down your top three fears. Leave space between each one.

3. Under each fear, write down why you're so fearful of that thing.

4. Once you have your list of fears and the reasons behind them, look up different Bible verses that speak to those fears.

5. Write those scriptures down and allow them to become your tool to combat those fears. Each time one of these fears tries to rise up, replace it with the scripture you have written.

Thought-Provoking Questions

1. Where does your fear originate?

_____

_____

_____

_____

2. Do you have proof to back up your fear?

_____

_____

_____

_____

Congratulations!

You have taken the 5th and final step towards
changing your life!
By now you should be feeling equipped!
You now have tools to help you overcome the
obstacles life throws at you. Use them as often as
you need to on your journey.

Love,
Dina M. Celestin

HEAL YOUR MIND, CHANGE YOUR LIFE LEADERS' GUIDE

The purpose for this guide is to provide tips to those who would like to lead a peer counseling group using this workbook as your guide.

Leaders, in order to be effective in your groups, you must first be willing to be transparent. Don't be ashamed; be open, honest, and willing to share your personal stories toward healing. It is advised that you read and go through the exercises, declarations, prayers, and questions on your own or in a group setting prior to leading a group. Keep in mind you can't give what you don't have.

Set the tone of the group, be clear of the purpose for the group, and make sure everyone participating has the same end goal of healing. As the leader, it's your responsibility to screen potential group members for their level of readiness for such a group.

Setting the Tone / Rules of the Group
Verbalize the following statements at the beginning of the first week.

1. This group is a safe place. All participants must know that this is a safe place to share, open up, ask for advice, or ask for prayer. I believe that true healing can occur only when those seeking healing feel safe and secure.

2. 2. Everything discussed in the group must be kept within the group. Anyone caught bad-mouthing someone else's

personal issues will be asked to leave the group until they are ready to pursue healing seriously.

3. All group members must be willing to be consistent with weekly group gatherings.

4. Have the contact information of a licensed counselor or therapist on hand whom you can refer people to who may need assistance beyond what the peer counseling group can offer.

5. Designate an assistant and/or prayer partner who can help you facilitate the group.

6. Questions are welcomed. But anything that may cause a disturbance in the group or overall healing of the other group members will be addressed after the group has been dismissed.

Sample Group Discussion Questions and Exercise

Week 1
You Are Enough

Sample Discussion Questions

1. Have you ever felt like you are not enough or that you don't have what it takes to achieve your goals?

2. Where do you think your feelings of inadequacy come from?

3. What are some techniques you've used to overcome the feelings of not being enough?

In-Person Exercise

Prior to your session, prepare a mirror that has strips of Velcro, and prepare a group of negative words and phrases that people typically think about themselves and a group of comforting words that God says about His children (also with Velcro on the back).

Examples of Negative Words and Phrases

- You're ugly.
- You're stupid.
- You're too fat.
- You're too skinny.
- You're too dark.
- You'll never make it.
- You're too white.
- You're crazy.

Examples of Positive Words and Phrases

- You are the head.
- You are loved.
- You are beautiful.
- You are handsome.
- You are strong.
- You are brave.
- You can do all things.
- You are blessed.
- You have a sound mind.

1. Have a volunteer come up and select the words and phrases from the negative group that they feel apply to them, and ask them to read them aloud.

2. Now blindfold the person and remove all the negative words from the mirror.

3. Replace the negative words with what God says about His children, and ask the person to read it aloud.

4. Ask the person to share how they feel after reading the positive words and phrases.

Week 2
Forgiveness

Sample Discussion Questions

1. What is one of the toughest things you've had to forgive someone for?

2. Do you believe that true forgiveness exists?

3. What myths have you heard about forgiveness?

4. How do you feel after reading this section about forgiveness?

5. Have you ever been in need of forgiveness?

6. How do you feel when someone says, "I forgive you"?

In-Person Exercise

1. Hold on to one end of a rope, and ask a group member to hold on to the other end as tight as they can.

2. Have the volunteer talk about a situation or a person they need to forgive.

3. As they speak, pull on your end of the rope, explain that the pulling represents their unforgiveness, and ask them how it feels to have something constantly pull at them.

4. Now have them let go of their end of the rope.

5. Ask them how they feel now that they have let the rope go. Confirm that they can choose to let go of unforgiveness the same way they let go of the rope, and they can feel freedom and relief internally.

Week 3
Letting Down Your Guard

Sample Discussion Questions

1. What are some situations when you feel like you need to keep your guard up?

2. What stops you from letting your guard down?

3. Do you feel like you've been able to create meaningful relationships while keeping your guard up?

In-Person Exercise

Prior to your session, set up a wall of faux bricks with a prize on the other end. (Your volunteer gets to keep the prize.)

Suggested Prizes

- gift cards
- inspirational book

- devotional
- bracelet
- earrings
- wallet
- small purse

1. Choose a volunteer to come up and knock down the faux brick wall.

2. Have them go get the prize behind the wall.

3. Ask them how they feel after knocking down the wall and getting their prize. Confirm that they would not have gotten this prize if they hadn't first knocked down the wall.

Week 4
How to Trust Again

Sample Discussion Questions

1. How can someone earn trust from others?

2. Does trust come easily for you, or does it take some time?

3. What are some ways someone can rebuild trust once it's been broken?

In-Person Exercise

Prior to your session, set up pipe halves, a small ball, and a small basket or box.

1. Ask five or six people to volunteer, and have them stand side by side with each holding a pipe half.

2. The object is to move the small ball from the beginning of the line to the end of the line.

3. Each person will hold a pipe half and use it to balance the ball until it passes into another person's pipe half. Then they move toward the end of the line so they can retake the ball when it reaches them again.

4. The object of the game is for the ball to end up in the basket or box.

> If the ball falls, you have to start again. Everyone wins in this game, and it encourages everyone to work together and trust each other.

Week 5
Living Fearlessly

Sample Discussion Questions

1. What are some things you're fearful of?

2. Does fear hinder you from reaching your personal goals?

3. Is it healthy to have a certain level of fear?

In-Person Exercise

1. Have everyone write the answers down to the questions above.

2. Then have them go through the Bible to find at least one bible scripture that will serve as a counterattack on those fears.

3. Then discuss as a group.

Tips

1. Instrumental worship and praise music can be played in the background during the exercise portion of the group.

2. Refreshments can be served.

3. Feel free to assign the questions found at the end of every chapter as homework for the following week.

4. Have willing group members share their responses to the questions at the beginning of each group. Willing group members can also briefly share their feelings after the exercise portion of the group, if time permits.

5. Always begin and end with a short word of prayer.

CLOSING REMARKS

You have everything you need to succeed already inside you, including the ability to self-heal through the power of God! The journey to the purposeful life you yearn to live starts with achieving wholeness; Through the power of healing your mind, which will lead to you ultimately changing your life. Without wholeness, everything you do is from a broken place and therefore tainted. Your life doesn't hold as much power when you're pouring out from a broken place. With the steps, exercises, prayers, and daily declarations in this book, you have gained the power to tap into your inner strength, which will help you conquer anything life tries to throw at you.

May this book bring you clarity on your journey toward healing.

Be blessed,
Dina M. Celestin

CLOSING PRAYER

Heavenly Father, thank You for the breath of life. Because of it we're able to receive daily opportunities to become the person you have created us to be. Without you, we would not be able to do this thing called life. Please help every reader walk boldly in the decision to become a better person. We give you full and total access to continue the healing and molding process in our lives.

In Jesus's name I pray. Amen.

Printed in the United States
by Baker & Taylor Publisher Services